VERTICAL TAKE-OFF
AIRCRAFT

Thanks to the creative team:

Senior Editor: Alice Peebles
Fact checking: Tom Jackson
Picture Research: Nic Dean
Design: 38a The Shop

First published in Great Britain in 2018
by Hungry Tomato Ltd
PO Box 181
Edenbridge
Kent, TN8 9DP
Copyright © 2018 Hungry Tomato Ltd

A CIP catalogue record for this book is
available from the British Library.

ISBN 978-1-912108-76-3

Printed and bound in China

Discover more at
www.hungrytomato.com

VERTICAL TAKE-OFF
AIRCRAFT

by Tim Harris

HUNGRY
TOMATO™

CONTENTS

Vertical Take-Off…	6
Search and Rescue	8
Military Helicopters	10
Jump Jets	12
Autogyros	14
Convertiplanes	16
Drones	18
Rockets	20
Lunar Modules	22
The Future	24
Record-breakers	26
Highlights of Flight	28
Glossary	30
Index	32

VERTICAL TAKE-OFF...

Aircraft that can take off and land vertically are sometimes described as VTOL (vertical take-off and landing) craft. Some have fixed wings, while others are powered by rotors. Many VTOL aircraft can hover.

▶ *In the hands of a skilled controller, a drone with an onboard camera can provide incredible footage of car races.*

Reaching the unreachable

The big advantage of VTOL aircraft is that they can take off and land in limited spaces. They don't need long runways. This means they are especially useful for reaching inaccessible places – in search-and-rescue operations, for example.

▶ *An injured climber is carried on a stretcher to a rescue helicopter.*

VTOL craft come in all shapes and sizes and are powered in different ways – some by jet or **internal combustion engines**, and others by rockets. Increasingly, engineers are developing electric craft to reduce noise and pollution. Read on to find out more.

Four forces

All aircraft, including helicopters, have four forces acting on them when they fly. Lift raises them off the ground, while gravity pulls them down. Thrust drives them forwards, and drag holds them back. For them to get airborne and move forwards, lift has to be greater than gravity, and thrust greater than drag.

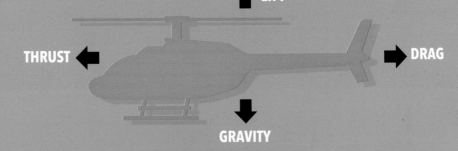

LIFT

THRUST

DRAG

GRAVITY

SEARCH AND RESCUE

Helicopters have one or two sets of spinning blades, or rotors, on top. These act like an aeroplane's wings. As the rotors spin, they create lift, the force that makes the helicopter rise.

Versatile transport

As well as the rotors on top, helicopters have a small rotor at the back. This helps to stabilize the helicopter by stopping the machine itself rotating as the main rotor spins. The pilot uses the main rotor to get the helicopter to move forwards, sideways – or even backwards! Helicopters can also hover, something that ordinary aircraft cannot do.

Search and rescue

Since they can move vertically up and down, helicopters don't need a runway to take off. This makes them perfect for landing in small areas. And because they can hover, they are ideal for rescuing people from sinking ships, burning buildings or rugged mountainsides.

◀ *An injured climber is rescued from the Prachov Rocks in the Czech Republic.*

Bigger and better

The first helicopters were flown in the 1930s. Since then, engineers have built bigger, faster and stronger machines. Helicopters are not used only for search and rescue. Many carry passengers, and others carry freight.

◄ This helicopter has to land in the yellow circle on an oil rig, which needs great piloting skill.

▲ A man is being winched to safety after an accident at sea.

The rotor

The helicopter's rotor mast leads to the **gearbox**. It spins very quickly and rotates the blades, or rotors. The swash plates translate commands from the pilot's controls to the rotor blades.

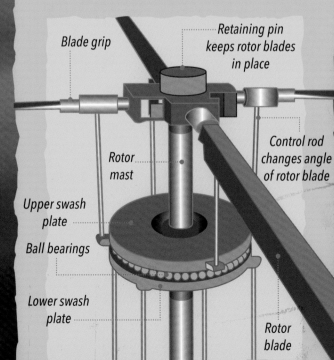

Blade grip

Retaining pin keeps rotor blades in place

Control rod changes angle of rotor blade

Rotor mast

Upper swash plate

Ball bearings

Lower swash plate

Rotor blade

MILITARY HELICOPTERS

Since World War II, helicopters have proved very useful in war zones. That is because they are versatile – able to land in small areas and on rough ground, unlike most aircraft.

Troop carrier

The Chinook CH-47 is probably the most successful troop-carrying helicopter of all time. It first flew in 1961 and many air forces, including the United States Air Force, still use it. The Chinook can carry heavy cargoes or up to 55 troops. It is a very fast vehicle, capable of 315 km/h (196 mph).

▲ The CH-47 has two sets of rotors so it can lift heavier loads.

Armoured design

Most military helicopters are used to carry troops or equipment. They are more heavily armoured than civilian helicopters, with extra protection given to the areas of the **fuselage** around the pilot, the engines and the fuel tanks. American Black Hawk helicopters have two engines, but if one is hit by enemy fire, they can fly on the other one. Some helicopters are designed to attack. They have guns mounted at the front and may carry rockets and missiles on **stub wings** at either side.

▶ *This combat helicopter has missiles under small 'wings' on either side of the fuselage.*

◀ *Because a helicopter can hover, the pilot is able to find the safest spot to land in bumpy terrain.*

JUMP JETS

Jump jets combine the vertical take-off and landing capabilities of helicopters with jet-powered speed, ideal for combat situations. A jump jet is designed to launch and land from the deck of a ship, a clearing in a forest or even from a city car park.

The thrust of the jet engines blasts through moveable **nozzles**. These are pointed towards the ground to push the aircraft into the air, then pointed backwards to drive the plane forwards. One of the most famous and successful jump jets was the Harrier. These operated from aircraft carriers, from where they flew on combat missions.

▲ *As well as taking off straight up into the air, the Sea Harrier could hover for up to five minutes.*

Vertical Lightning

One of the latest VTOL aircraft is the American F-35B Lightning II. A nozzle at the end of the exhaust and two nozzles under the wings provide downward thrust when the plane is lifting off or landing vertically.

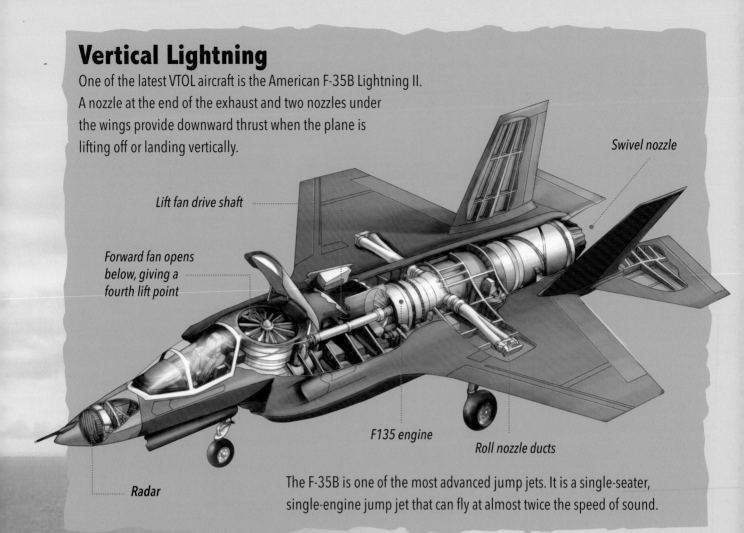

Lift fan drive shaft

Swivel nozzle

Forward fan opens below, giving a fourth lift point

F135 engine

Roll nozzle ducts

Radar

The F-35B is one of the most advanced jump jets. It is a single-seater, single-engine jump jet that can fly at almost twice the speed of sound.

The undercarriage of this F-35B Lightning has been lowered as the plane prepares to land.

AUTOGYROS

Autogyros have horizontal rotors to provide lift, and vertical rotors to give forward motion. The vertical rotors are driven by an engine, but the horizontal rotors – unlike a helicopter's – are turned by the craft's forward movement through the air.

For an autogyro to lift off the ground vertically, its horizontal rotors must be able to spin quickly. This is done by tip jets: small rockets at the ends of the rotors. When these fire, the rotors spin around, a bit like a Catherine wheel firework.

A spinning Catherine wheel in fiery motion

An autogyro can do many of the things that a helicopter can, but at a fraction of the cost in fuel.

Take-off

The tip jets only operate during take-off and landing so the autogyro doesn't use much fuel. When it's flying forwards, the motion through the air turns the rotors and keeps it airborne.

▲ *This autogyro can fly a pilot and a passenger.*

Heliplanes

Engineers are developing a new kind of vertical take-off autogyro called a heliplane. Its free-spinning rotor has tip jets at each end. These are driven with air from two **propulsion engines**. The heliplane will be able to cruise at twice the speed of a normal helicopter and travel long distances.

▲ *An artist's impression of the heliplane design from the USA's Defense Advanced Research Projects Agency*

CONVERTIPLANES

Imagine you were on a rescue mission to find some people lost in the jungle, in an area too far away for a helicopter to reach and where there were no aircraft runways. If only your team had a plane that could fly to the area like a normal plane, then stop, hover and descend vertically into a small forest clearing…

Well, such aircraft do exist! Meet the Boeing V-22 Osprey. When flying horizontally, it is just like an ordinary propeller plane, but it can descend to the ground vertically by switching the rotors through 90 degrees. These are called tiltrotors, which describes just what they do.

The Osprey can also perform this trick the other way around, taking off like a helicopter and then moving the rotors again to fly like a normal plane.

Tiltrotors

Both of Osprey's tiltrotors can move through 90 degrees to convert it from a normal plane to a helicopter.

▶ *This sequence shows how Osprey's tiltrotors change from vertical to horizontal.*

The Osprey

The Boeing V-22 Osprey can take off from, or land in, an open space not much larger than itself. It can climb hundreds of metres vertically to get out of a deep canyon. The Osprey can carry four crew and 32 troops, or 9 tonnes (10 US tons) of cargo.

▲ *This Osprey is ready to land, wth its rotors spinning horizontally and its wheels down.*

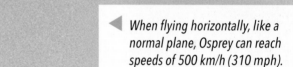

◄ *When flying horizontally, like a normal plane, Osprey can reach speeds of 500 km/h (310 mph).*

DRONES

Drones are unmanned aerial vehicles. They were originally designed and built for the military to perform missions considered too dull, dirty or dangerous for humans to do.

Small drones are powered by batteries, and larger ones by aircraft engines. A human operator pilots their direction, altitude and speed by remote control, or they are controlled by an onboard computer.

◀ *Modern drones are ideal for filming hard-to-reach places such as glaciers. The camera on this Phantom 4 can film forwards, backwards, sideways and down.*

Multi-purpose machines

Drones are used to deliver packages and to film and photograph crowds, places and sports events. They are sometimes raced against each other. Military drones are used for spying missions and dropping supplies in dangerous combat zones. Drones are sometimes fitted with sensors to measure pollution in the atmosphere. Onboard computers control and record speed, altitude and direction of flight.

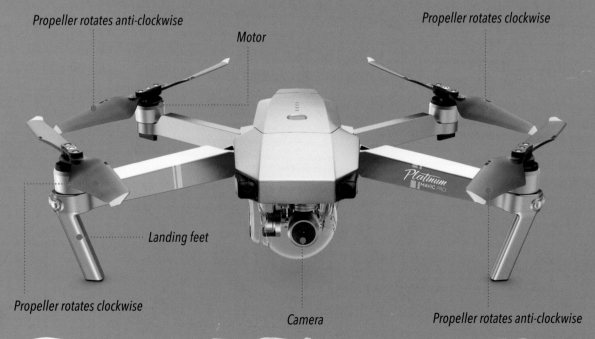

Propeller rotates anti-clockwise

Motor

Propeller rotates clockwise

Landing feet

Propeller rotates clockwise

Camera

Propeller rotates anti-clockwise

Saving time

Drones can save precious time in searches for missing animals. When a puppy fell down a cliff and was lost just before nightfall, a drone was flown to the area to search for it. Once the drone had located the unlucky animal, rescuers knew exactly where to look. They found the puppy alive and well. Other drones have found missing persons.

▲ *The Phantom 4 has been designed for precise handling. It can hover over an exact spot, so is ideal for filming wild animals such as nesting birds.*

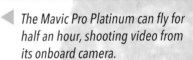

◄ *The Mavic Pro Platinum can fly for half an hour, shooting video from its onboard camera.*

Beach patrol

This drone flies above a beach resort, carrying a flotation device. If someone gets into difficulty while swimming, the drone flies over to them and drops the lifebuoy nearby.

▲ *This German 'rescue drone' can fly at 65 km/h (40 mph).*

ROCKETS

Rockets work by blasting the exhaust gases from burning fuel at high speed in one direction. This thrusts the rocket in the opposite direction.

Rockets were invented in China hundreds of years ago. Modern rockets are used as fireworks, weapons and vehicles for space exploration. In fact, they are the only way to launch heavy spacecraft into orbit, nearly 100 kilometres (62 miles) above Earth. This is the edge of space, above which jet engines will not work.

Launch time

The Apollo 11 mission took astronauts to the Moon in 1969. They flew in a **module** near the top of the giant Saturn V rocket, and left Earth's gravity after 2 hours 44 minutes.

▲ A Saturn V rocket launches the Apollo 11 mission on 16 July 1969.

Into space

The USA's Apollo missions used Saturn V rockets to carry astronauts almost 400,000 kilometres (250,000 miles) to the Moon's orbit. The rockets had to be extremely powerful to achieve that. Each Saturn V rocket took off vertically from its launch pad at Cape Canaveral, Florida. It carried enough liquid hydrogen and oxygen fuel to drive a car 800 times around Earth.

▲ (left to right) Neil Armstrong, Michael Collins and 'Buzz' Aldrin, the Apollo 11 astronauts who reached the Moon in 1969

Each Saturn V was taller than the Statue of Liberty in New York. At take-off, when full of fuel, the rocket weighed more than 400 elephants. A Saturn V also launched the American **Skylab** space station in 1973. It orbited Earth until 1979.

Reusable rocket

The Falcon 9 rockets carry satellites and other hardware into orbit around Earth. Unlike the Saturn Vs, which were abandoned in space, Falcon 9 returns to Earth after each mission, using legs to stabilize itself as it lands.

▶ Falcon 9 coming down to land, exhaust flaring

LUNAR MODULES

The most dramatic vertical landings and take-offs of all carried astronauts on to and off the surface of the Moon. But while the astronauts are remembered, the craft that got them there aren't so well-known.

▶ *Lunar Module in flight*

When National Aeronautics and Space Administration (NASA) scientists were planning the Apollo 11 Moon mission in 1969, they faced a big problem: how to transport astronauts from the **Command Module** (which had carried them most of the way to the Moon) to the Moon's surface. NASA came up with the brilliant idea of a **Lunar Module** (LM), which would separate from the parent craft (the Command Module) and make a safe landing.

The Lunar Module separated from the Command Module, and its own small rocket engine propelled it to the Moon's surface. The Lunar Module had four legs with foot pads to give it a soft landing. When Neil Armstrong and Buzz Aldrin touched down in the Lunar Module, they became the first men on the Moon. They had made the most famous landing ever!

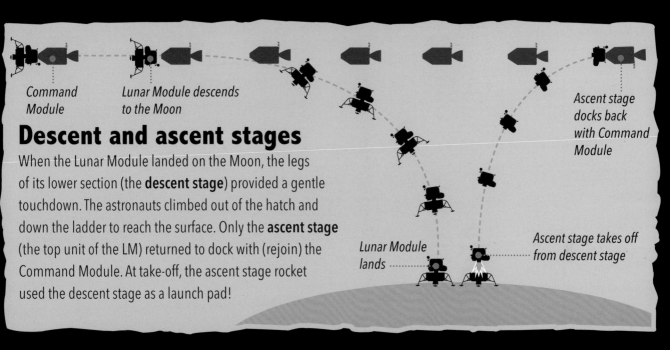

Command Module

Lunar Module descends to the Moon

Ascent stage docks back with Command Module

Ascent stage takes off from descent stage

Lunar Module lands

Descent and ascent stages

When the Lunar Module landed on the Moon, the legs of its lower section (the **descent stage**) provided a gentle touchdown. The astronauts climbed out of the hatch and down the ladder to reach the surface. Only the **ascent stage** (the top unit of the LM) returned to dock with (rejoin) the Command Module. At take-off, the ascent stage rocket used the descent stage as a launch pad!

Relinking in orbit

While the Lunar Module and its astronauts were on the Moon, the Command Module, with its own pilot, was orbiting about 100 kilometres (62 miles) overhead. When the time came to return home, the astronauts climbed into the LM's ascent stage. This had its own rocket engine, which didn't need to be powerful because it was only fighting the Moon's weak gravity. The ascent stage launched vertically, and within a short time, was reunited with the Command Module – and the long journey back to Earth was underway.

▲ Astronaut Buzz Aldrin walks on the Moon, the Lunar Module 'Eagle' in the background.

THE FUTURE

What might the VTOL aircraft of the future be like? With fears about fossil fuels such as oil running out, aircraft engineers are studying ways to limit their use, particularly by designing faster, quieter and cleaner aircraft powered by electricity.

The Sikorsky Firefly is an all-electric helicopter with a motor powered by two batteries. The Firefly can reach a top speed of almost 150 km/h (92 mph), but there is only room for the pilot. It can remain airborne for 15 minutes.

Greased Lightning

Imagine a pilotless drone that can take off and land vertically like other drones, but can also fly like a small plane. Well, that's Greased Lightning, built and flown by NASA engineers. It has 10 battery-powered engines and a wingspan of 6.1 metres (20 feet) . With the wings pointed up, it takes off and lands like a helicopter. Once airborne, the wings and engines tilt forward, making it much faster through the air. Greased Lightning will be able to do everything that other drones do – but quicker than most.

▲ *Eight of Greased Lightning's engines are on the wing, with two more on the horizontal stabilizer at the rear.*

Engineers are developing faster and quieter helicopters, such as this twin-rotor Sikorsky X2.

The Puffin

NASA is developing the Puffin, a single-person, electric aircraft that will take off and land vertically. Since Puffin will get its energy from batteries, it will not produce polluting gases and will be very quiet.

▶ *The Puffin's designers hope that it will be able to fly at 240 km/h (150 mph).*

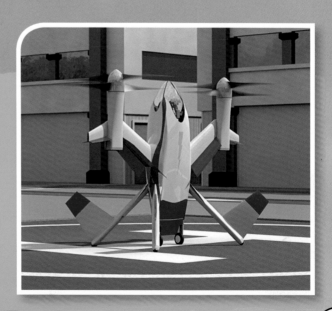

RECORD-BREAKERS

In May 2013, a climber was injured on Mount Everest, 7,800 metres (25,600 feet) up. He needed help – fast.

Then Italian helicopter pilot Simone Moro lifted him to safety – saving his life in the highest helicopter rescue mission ever. In fact, VTOL craft have set many records.

Giant helicopter

The Russian Mi-26 military transport helicopter needs an eight-blade rotor with a diameter of 32 metres (105 feet) to lift it off the ground. Fully laden, its take-off weight is 100 tonnes (110 US tons), about the same as eight double-decker buses.

Tallest rocket

The Saturn V rocket that sent astronauts to the Moon was 111 metres (363 feet) tall and 10 metres (33 feet) in diameter. Now NASA plans to build an even bigger rocket to launch astronauts further into space.

Highest helicopter flight

French test pilot Jean Boulet, flying an Aérospatiale SA 315 Lama, broke the altitude record for a helicopter when he reached a height of 12,442 metres (40,820 feet) in 1972.

Fastest jump jet

The French air force's Mirage jump jet has a top speed of twice the speed of sound: about 2,500 km/h (1,550 mph).

In 1999, an Mi-26 transported a 25-tonne (27.5-US ton) block of frozen soil and the remains of a 23,000-year-old woolly mammoth!

Longest flight

A Sikorsky helicopter was the first to cross the Atlantic Ocean: 6,870 kilometres (4,270 miles) from New York to Paris in over 30 hours. It was a bit of a cheat, though, because the 'copter was refuelled nine times by an accompanying aircraft.

HIGHLIGHTS OF FLIGHT

People imagined aircraft that would take off vertically long before the technology was invented to make it happen. Sometimes they wrote stories about such flying machines, and even drew them.

1936

The Focke Wulf was the first helicopter capable of **sustained** flight with a pilot at the controls. Two years later, it flew 230 kilometres (143 miles).

2000 BCE

A Chinese legend tells the story of Wan Hu, an official of the Ming Dynasty, who was shot into space attached to rockets. The first rockets were actually made more than 3,000 years later.

15th century

Leonardo da Vinci sketched an '**aerial** screw', which, he thought, might lift into the air if it were spun. The machine was never built, however.

▶ *This VTOL fighter jet first flew for the RAF in 1978, and entered service with the Royal Navy two years later.*

1969

A Saturn V rocket launched the first astronauts to land on the Moon.

1996

The Boeing Sikorsky RAH-66 was the most advanced combat helicopter, but it was too expensive to enter service.

1980

The Sea Harrier jump jet entered service with the British Royal Navy.

2017

The German-engineered Lilium personal jet was the first vertical take-off and landing electric jet for private use.

GLOSSARY

aerial in flight

ascent stage the upper section of the Lunar Module, which carried astronauts Neil Armstrong and Buzz Aldrin back from the Moon's surface to the Command Module

Command Module the section of the Apollo 11 spacecraft used by the crew and designed to return to Earth

descent stage the legs and landing pads of the Lunar Module that landed astronauts on the Moon; this detachable lower section remained behind after the landing

fuselage the main body of an aircraft

gearbox set of gears in an engine; these interlocking cogged wheels turn at different rates to control a vehicle's speed

internal combustion engine an engine that generates power by burning fuel and air, producing hot gases that drive machinery

Lunar Module two-man spacecraft, part of the Apollo 11 mission that made the historic 1969 Moon landing possible

module self-contained unit of a spacecraft, from which the craft can separate

nozzle spout at the end of a tube used to control a jet of gas

propulsion engine a machine that produces thrust to push an aircraft forward; in a heliplane, for example, the propulsion is provided by jet engines

radar long-range system for detecting objects using radio waves; short for **RA**dio **D**etection **A**nd **R**anging

Skylab the USA's only space station to date; this NASA project carried out experiments and research aboard a section of an enormous Saturn V rocket, which was converted to contain living quarters and a workshop for the three-man crews

stub wings short wings that are used to support machinery, rather than for flight

sustained continuing for an extended period of time

versatile able to change easily from one activity to another

▶ *An emergency worker guides the approach of a search-and-rescue Airbus helicopter.*

INDEX

A
Apollo 11 moon mission
  20–23
autogyros 14–15

B
beach patrols 19
Black Hawk helicopter 10

C
Chinook CH-47 11
convertiplanes 16–17

D
drones 18–19, 24

E
electric aircraft 24–25

F
F35 Lightning 12, 13
Falcon 9 21
future VTOL aircraft 24–25

G
Greased Lightning 24

H
Harrier Jump Jet 12, 13
helicopter rotor 9
helicopters 8, 9, 26, 27
  electric 24
  military 10–11, 26
  search-and-rescue 8–9
heliplanes 15

J
jump jets 12–13, 27

L
lunar modules 22–23

M
Mi-26 helicopter 26
military helicopters 10–11, 26
Mirage jump jet 27

P
Puffin 25

R
record-breakers 26–27
rockets 20–21, 26

S
Saturn V rockets 20, 21, 26
search and rescue 8, 19, 26
Sikorsky Firefly 24

T
tiltrotors 16, 17

V
V-22 Osprey 16, 17

The Author

Tim Harris lives in London and loves the natural world, science and travel. He has written many children's and adults' books for Bloomsbury, Dorling Kindersley, National Geographic and Grolier. His subjects include the history of engineering, animal anatomy, great battles, meteorology and geography. Tim has also edited several travel guides, and before entering the world of book publishing, he was deputy editor of *Birdwatch* magazine.

Picture credits (abbreviations: t = top; b = bottom; c = centre; l = left; r = right)

1 = AirSeaLand Photos. 2 = Mavic Pro. 3 = Shutterstock. 4/5 = AirSeaLand Photos. 6, b = AirSeaLand Photos6/7 = DJI Drones. 8, b = ShutterStock. 8/9, c = AirSeaLand Photos. 9, t = ShutterStock. 10, l = AirSeaLand Photos. 10/11, c = AirSeaLand Photos11, b = AirSeaLand Photos, 12, b = AirSeaLand Photos.12/13, c = AirSeaLand Photos. 14/15, c = Aypics/Alamy Stock Photo. 15, t = Shutterstock. 15, b = Wikipedia. 16/17 = AirSeaLand Photos. 16/17, b = AirSeaLand Photos. 17, t = ShutterStock. 18, tl = Mavic Pro. 18, b = Mavic Pro. 18/19, c = Mavic Pro. 19, t = Mavic Pro. 19, b = dpa picture alliance/Alamy Stock Photo20, l = NASA/Apollo Launch 2 Photo. 20/21 = Alamy. 21, tr = Photo Spacex-crs7-launch. 21, br = NASA. 22, c = ShutterStock. 23, br = Images/Alamy Stock Photo. 24, l = NASA. 24/25, c = ShutterStock. 25, br = NASA. 26, l = NASA. 26/27 = Stocktrek Images/ Alamy Stock Photo. 27, r = AirSeaLand Photos. 27, b = Wikipedia. 28/29 = ShutterStock. 31 = Shutterstock. 32 = Shutterstock.